Antique Botanical

Art

&

Inspirations

Volume 1

Carol Graham

ISBN: 97988652668100

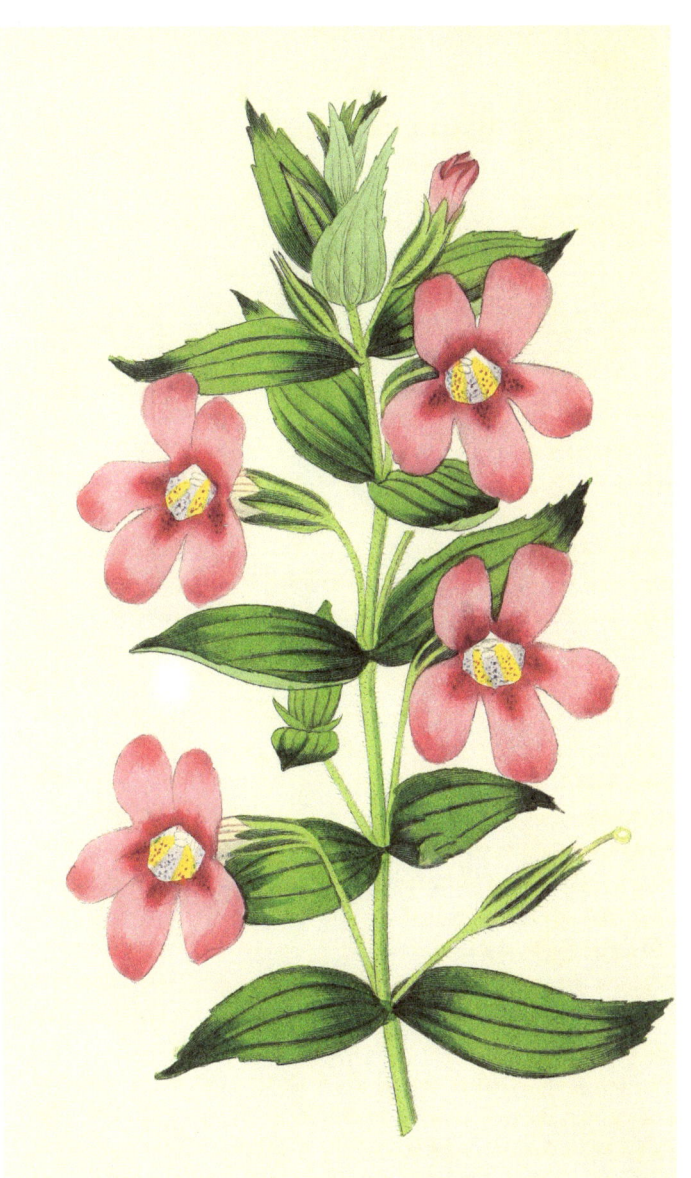

Mimulus roseus.

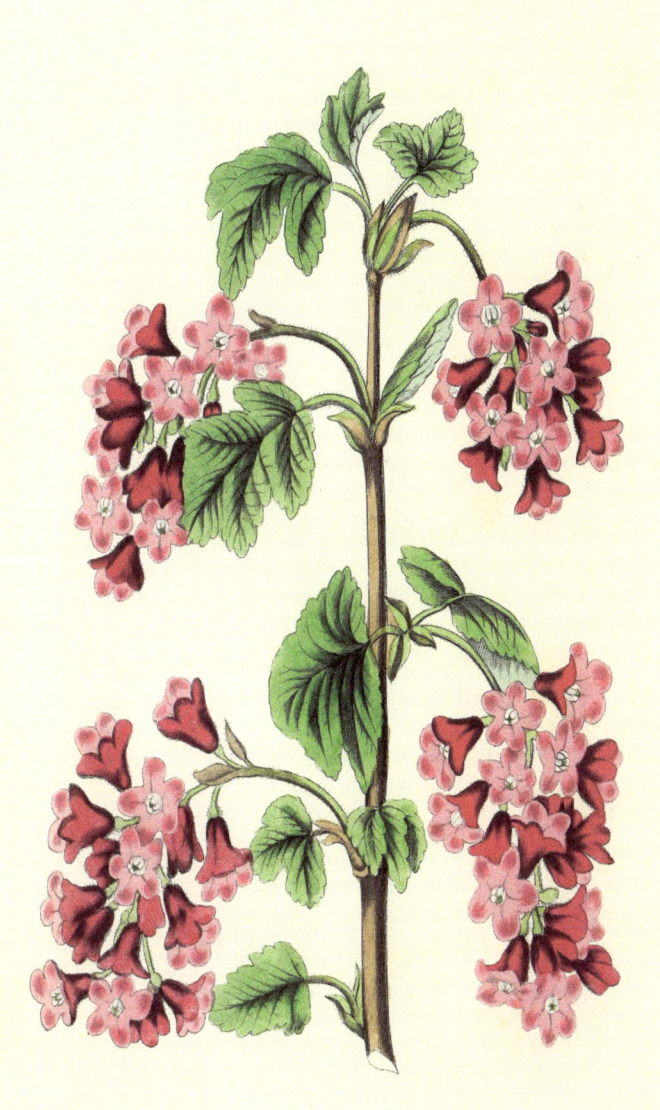

Ribes sanguineum

FEB. 1834.

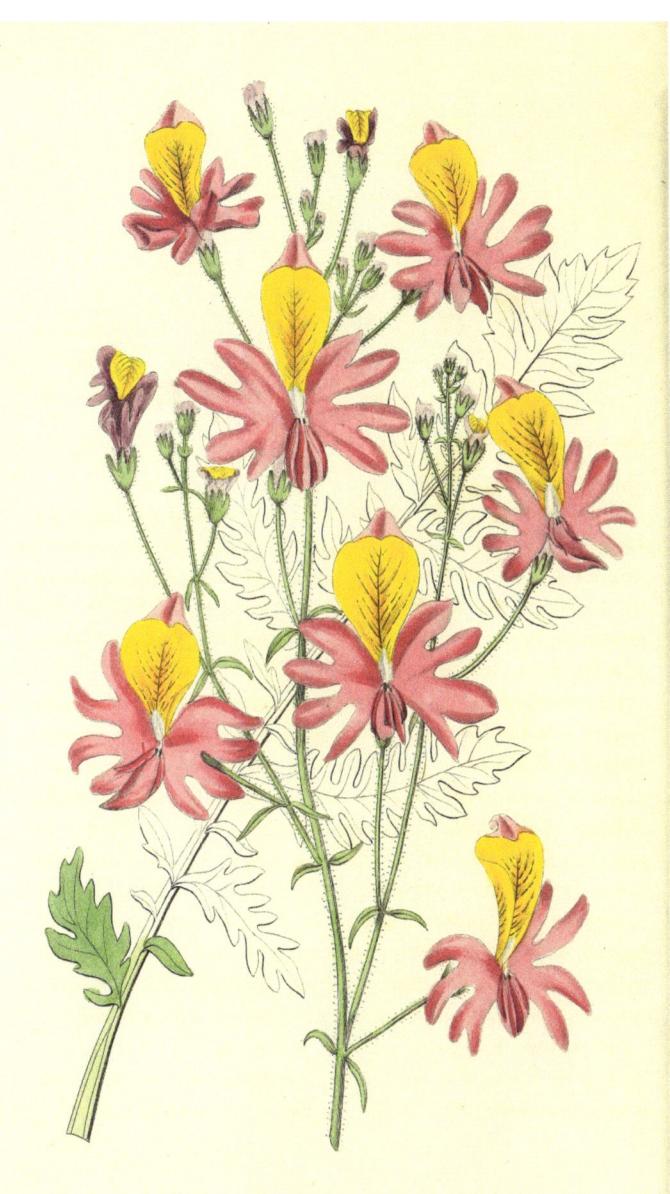

Schizanthus retusus.

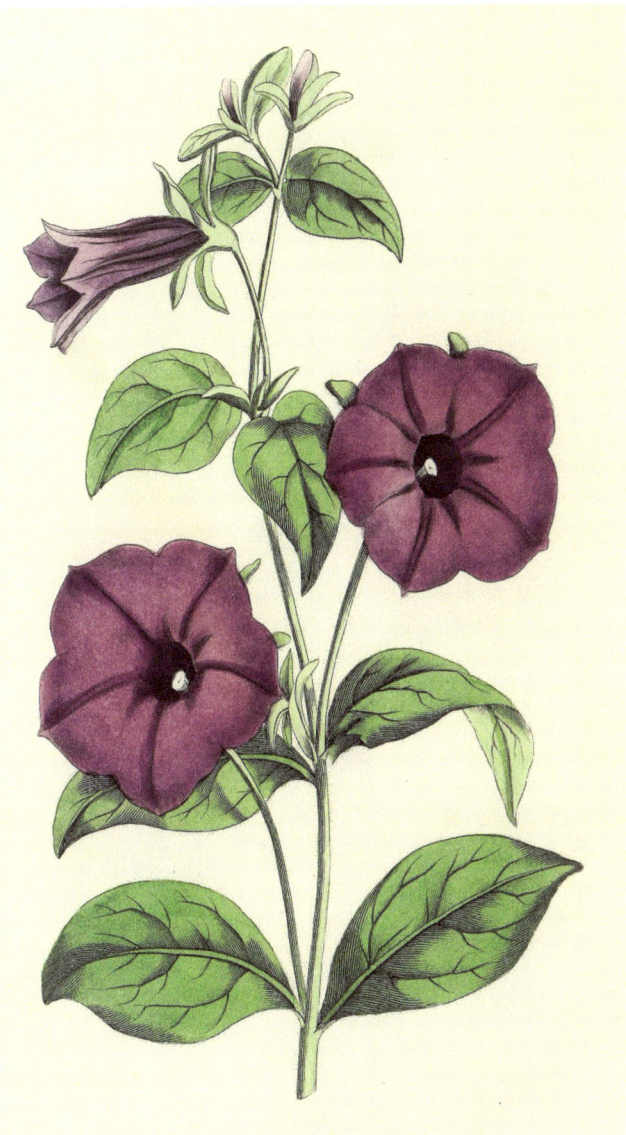

Petunia violacea.

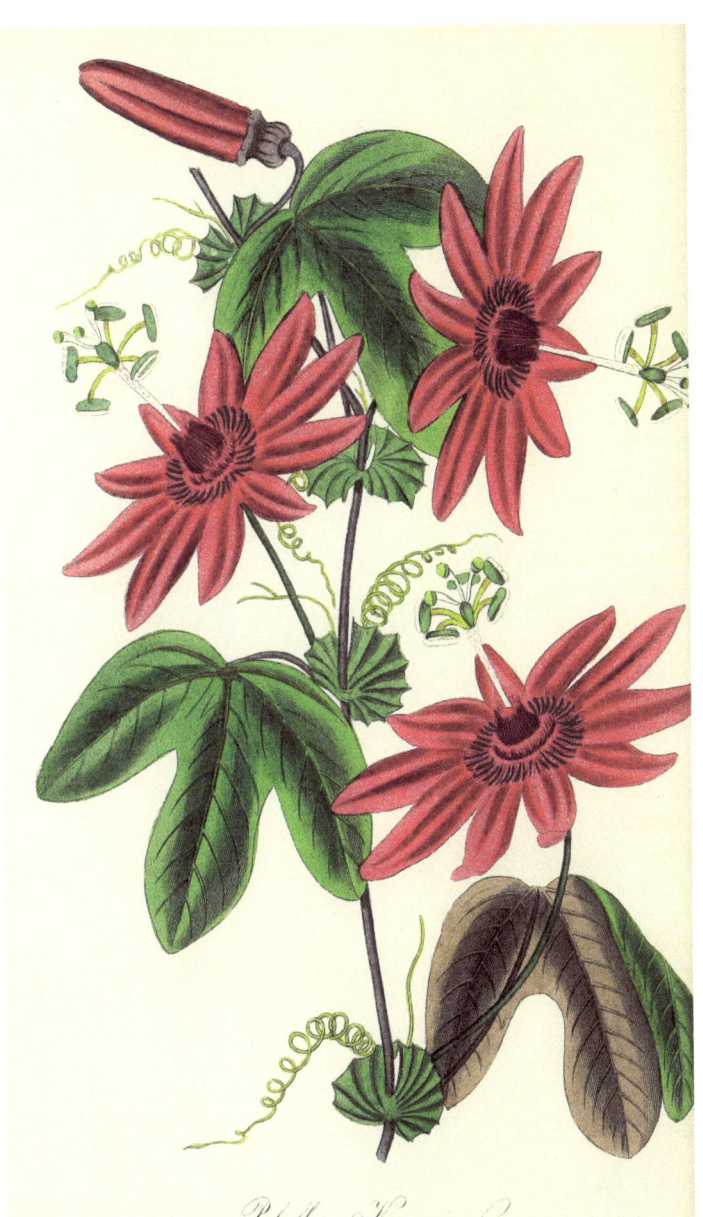

Passiflora Kermesina

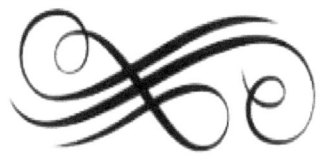

Actions vs Words

Actions prove who

someone is,

Words just prove who they

want to be.

Unknown

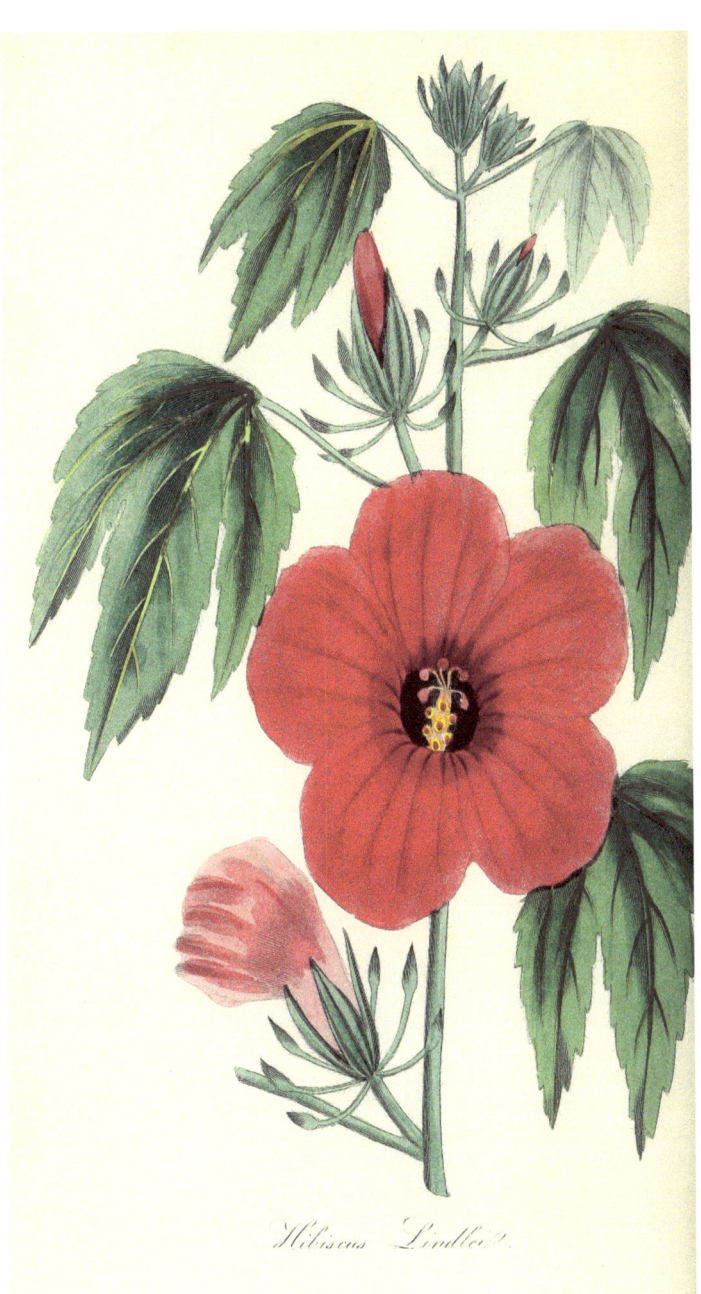

Hibiscus Lindlei.

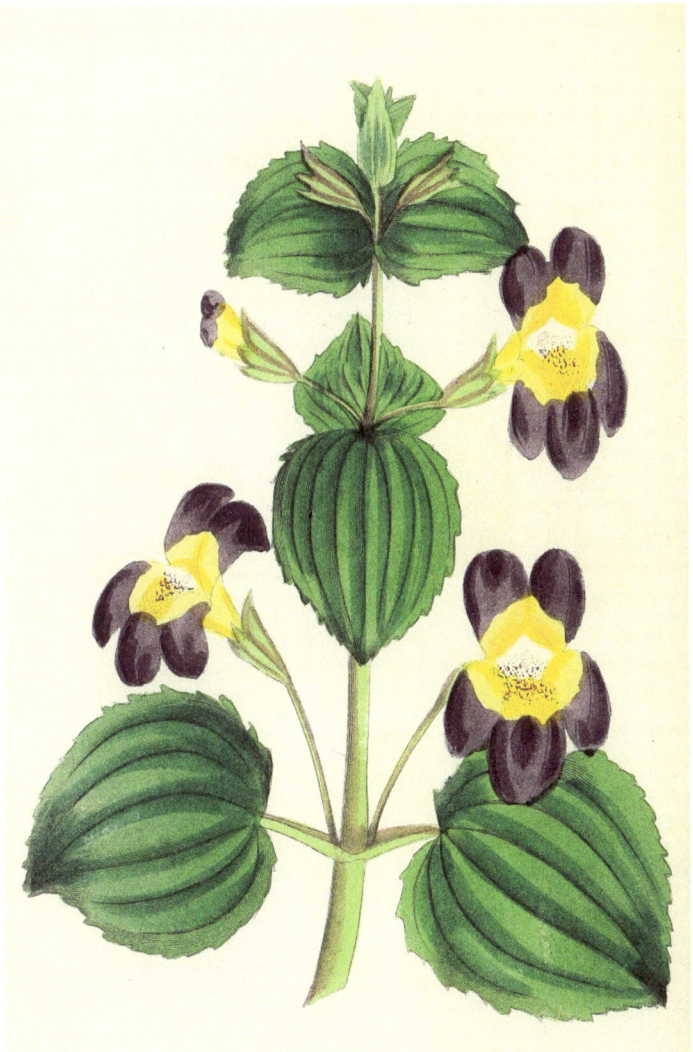

Mimulus variegatus.

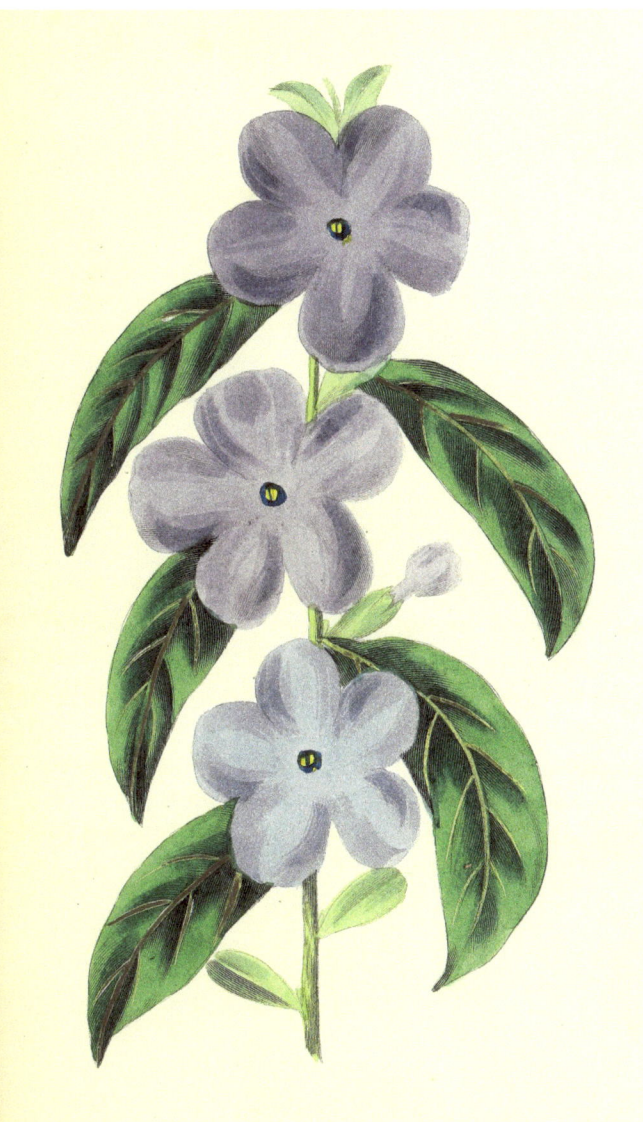

Franciscea Hopeana?

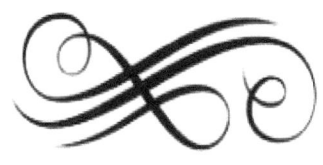

Bad vs. Good

Sometimes the bad things
that happen in our lives leads
us directly on the path to the
best things that will ever
happen in our lives.

Unknown

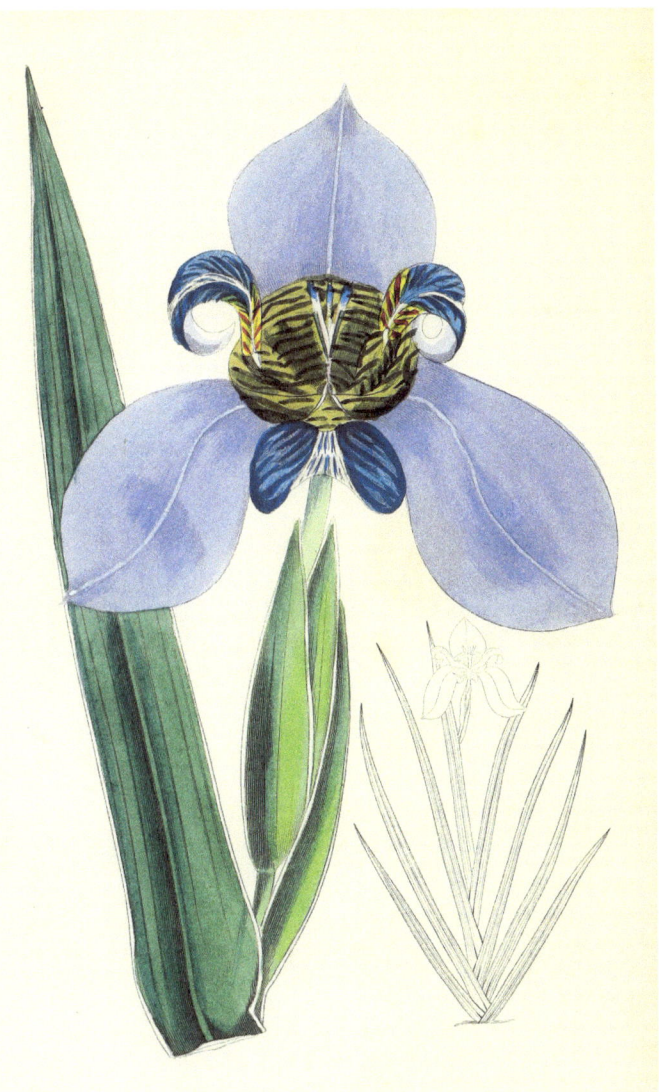

Marica Sabini.

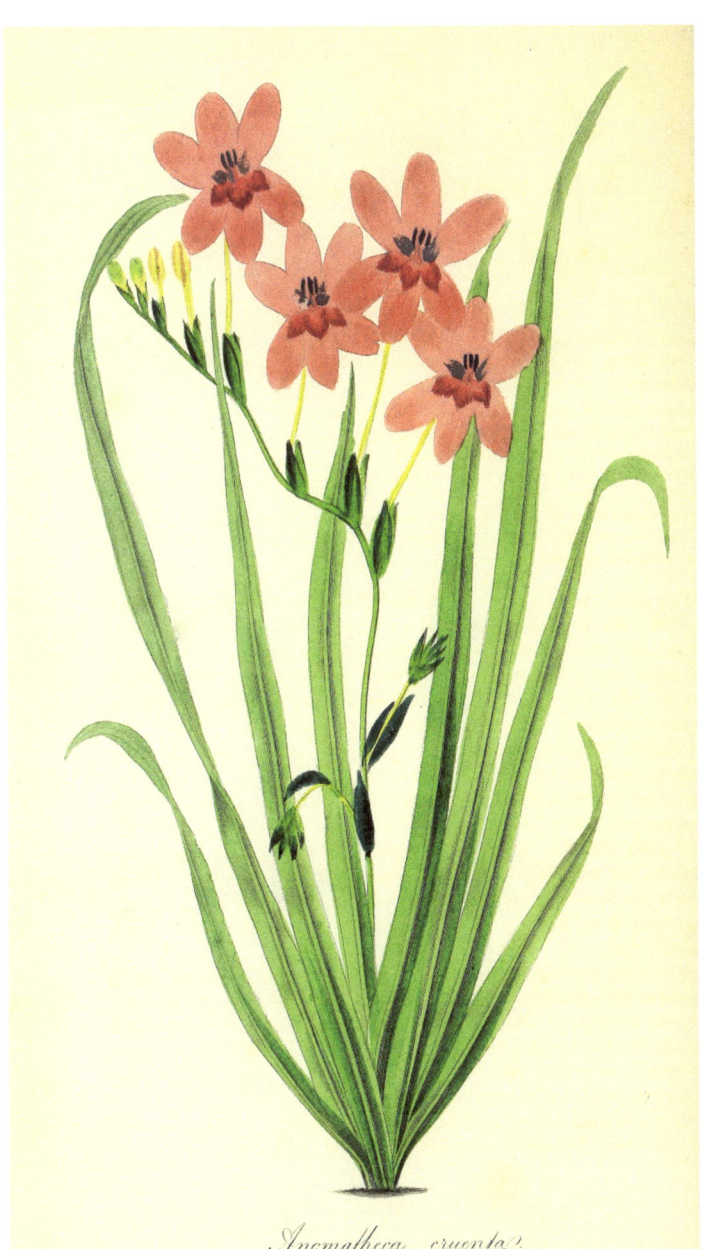

Anomatheca cruenta.

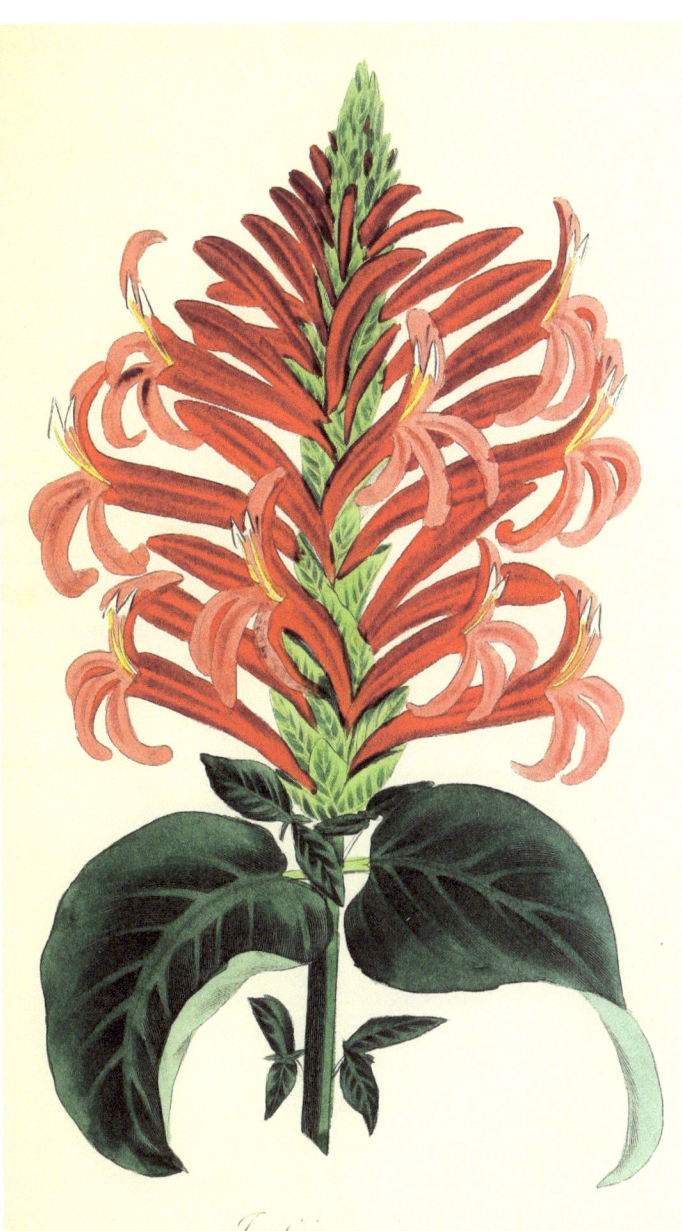

Justicia coccinea

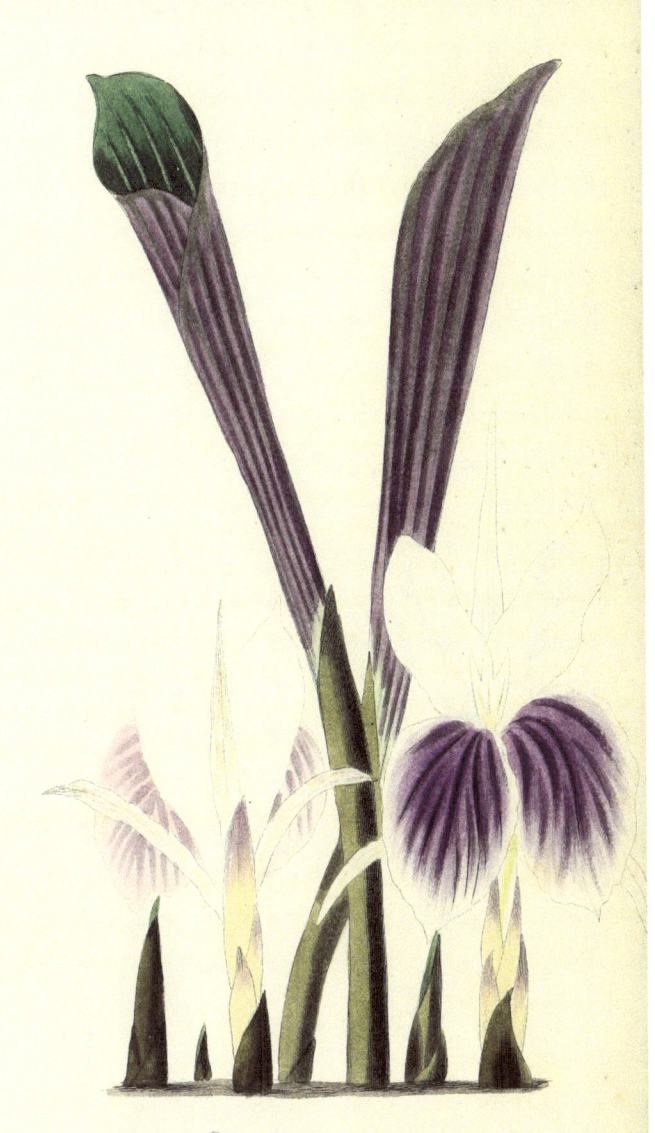

Kæmpferia rotunda?

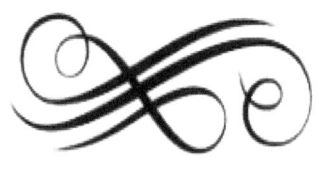

Because

I love you not because of what you have
but because of what I feel.
I care about you not because you need
care but because I want to.
I am always here for you not because
I want you to be with me but because
I want to be with you.

Unknown

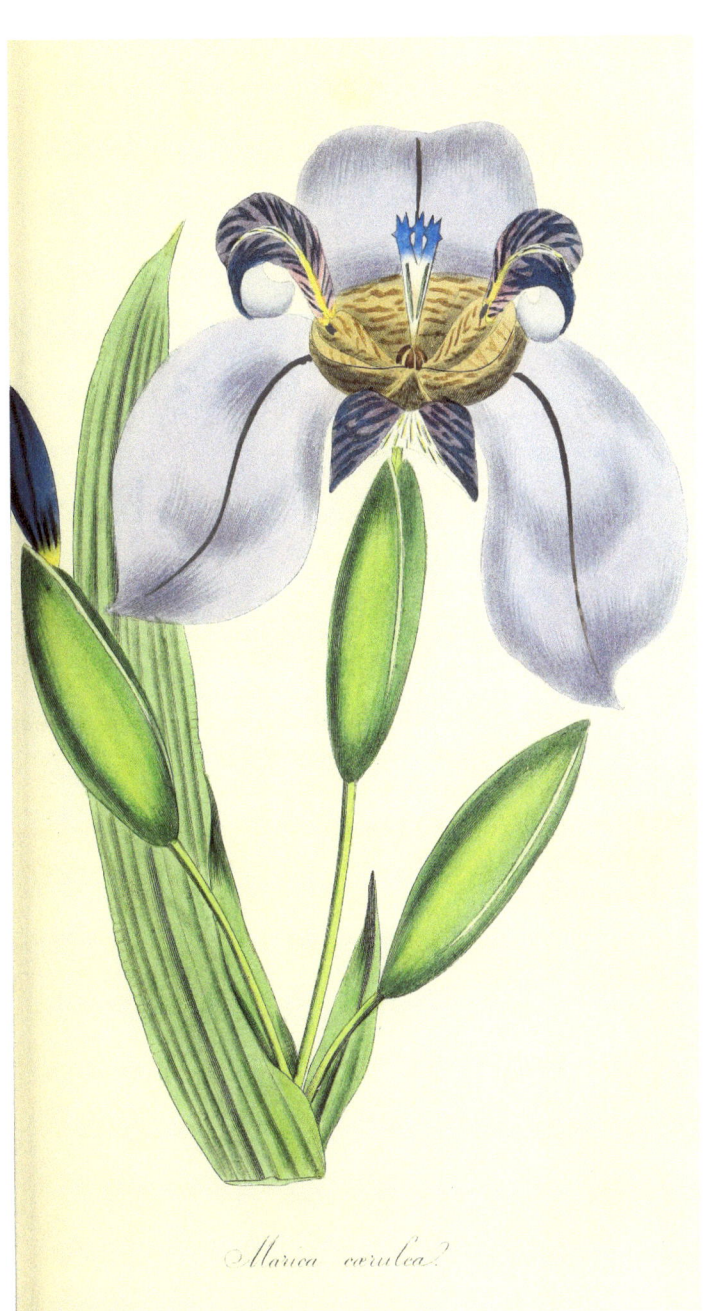

Marica cærulea?

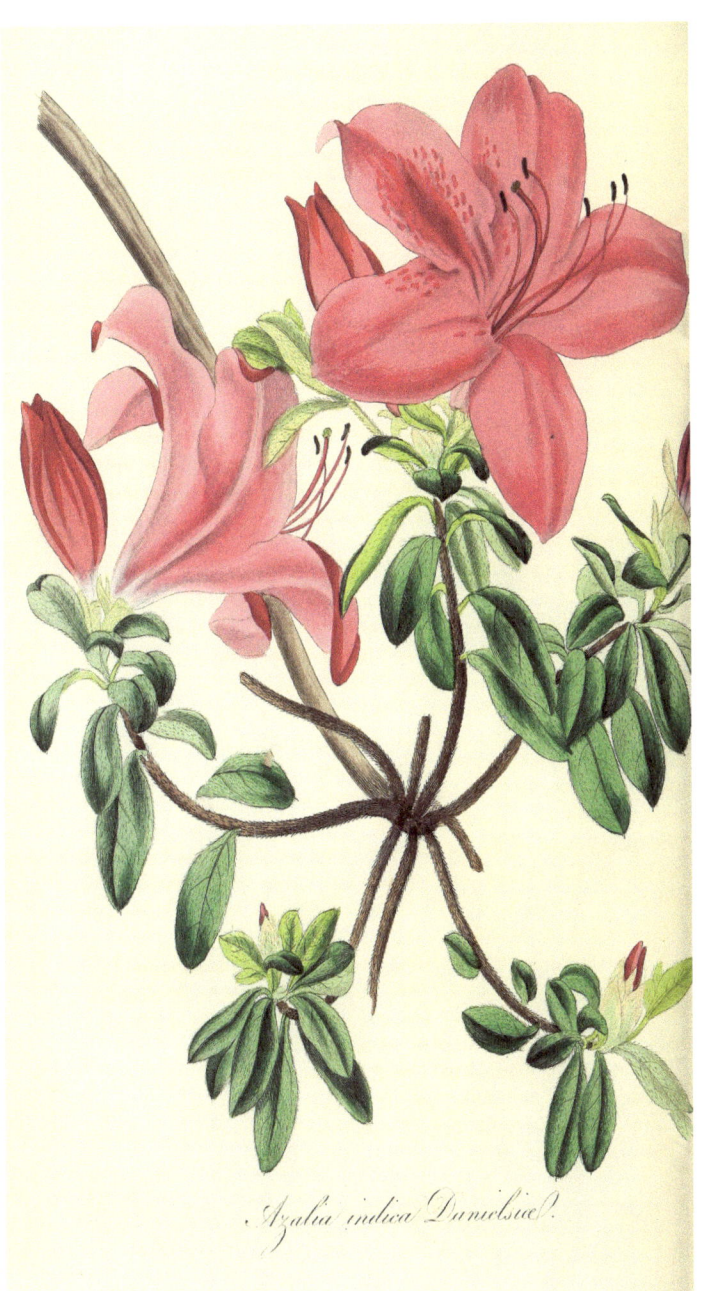

Azalia indica Danielsiæ.

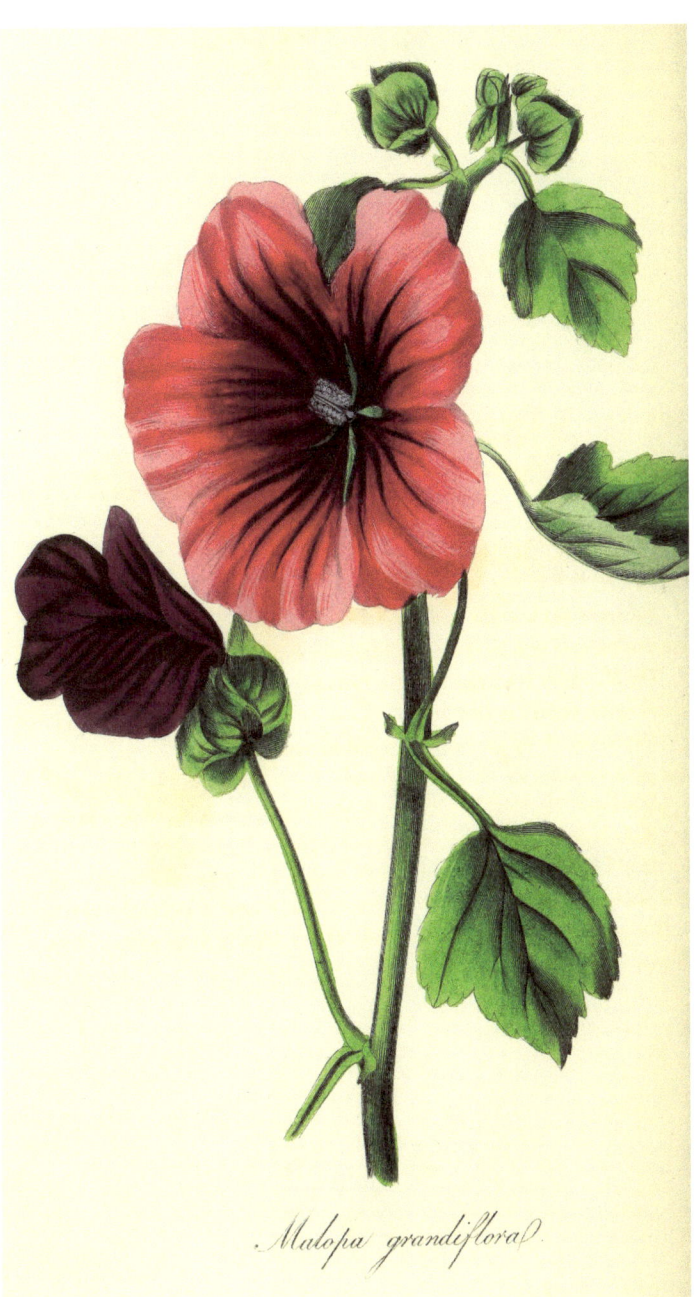

Malopa grandiflora.

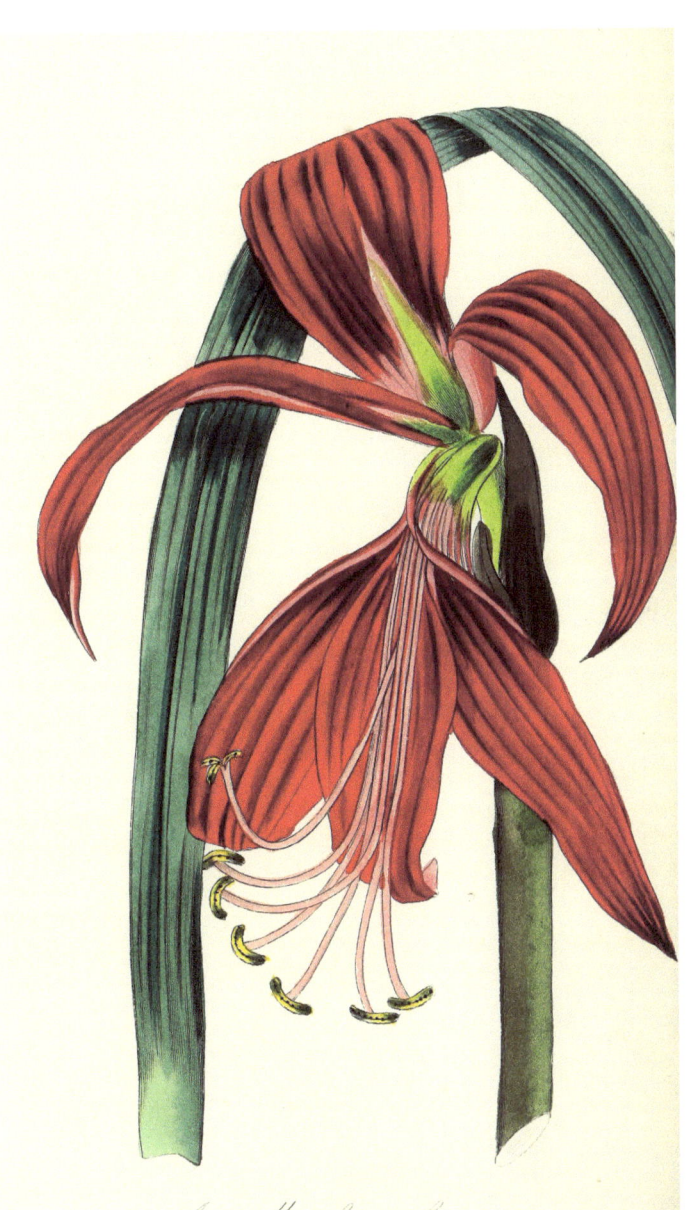

Amaryllis formosissima

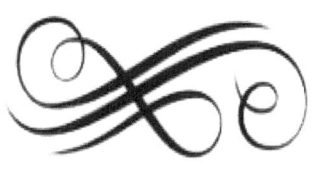

Control

Don't let yourself be controlled
by three things:

People

Money

Past Experiences

Unknown

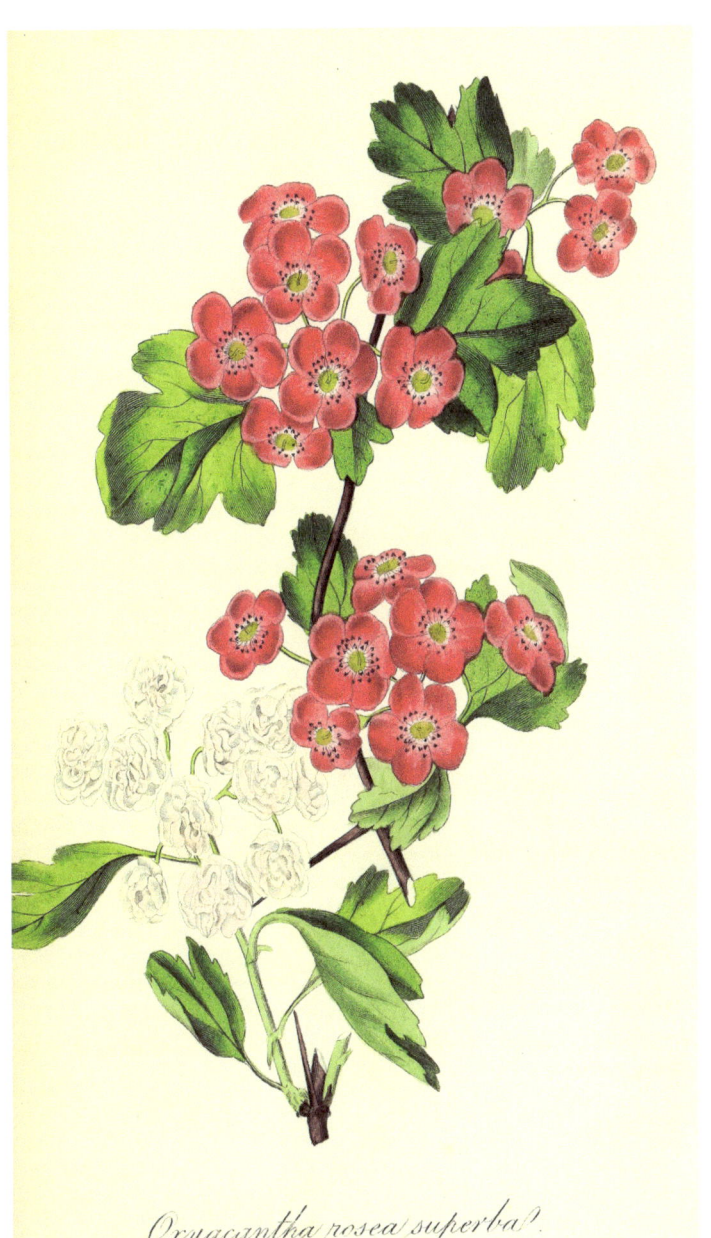

Oxyacantha rosea superba.

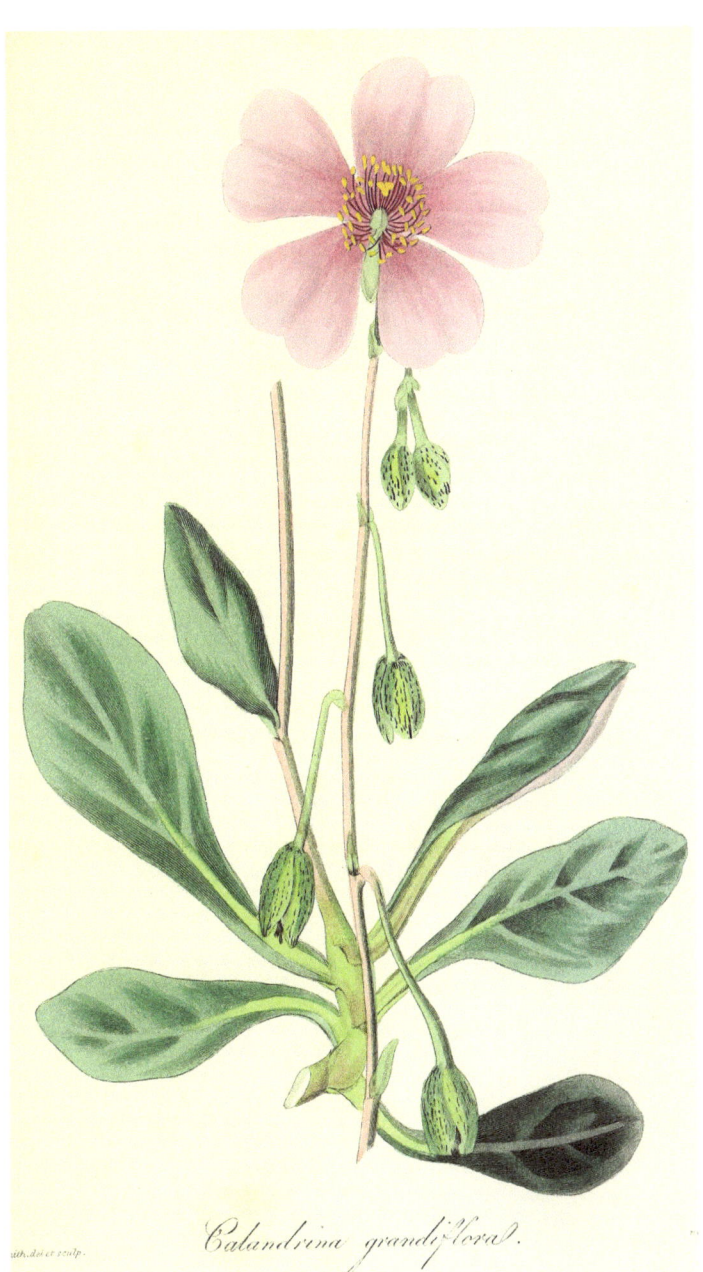

Calandrina grandiflora.

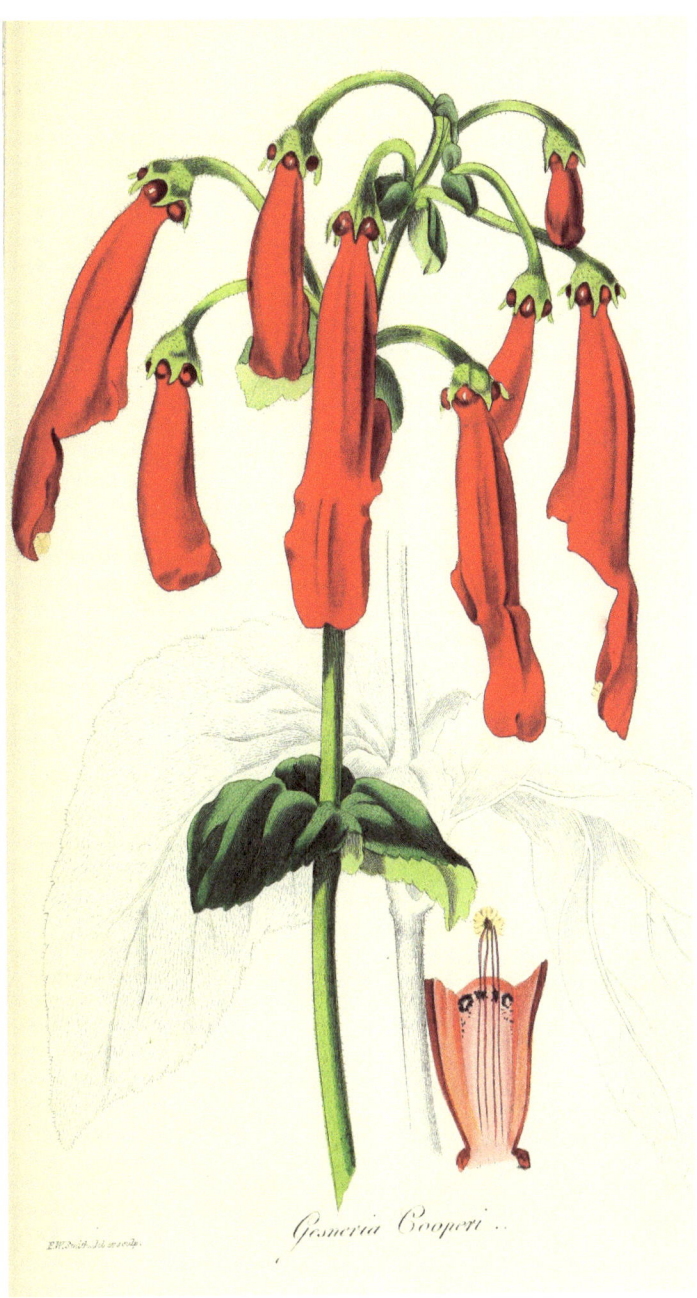

Gesneria Cooperi.

E.W.Smith del et lith.

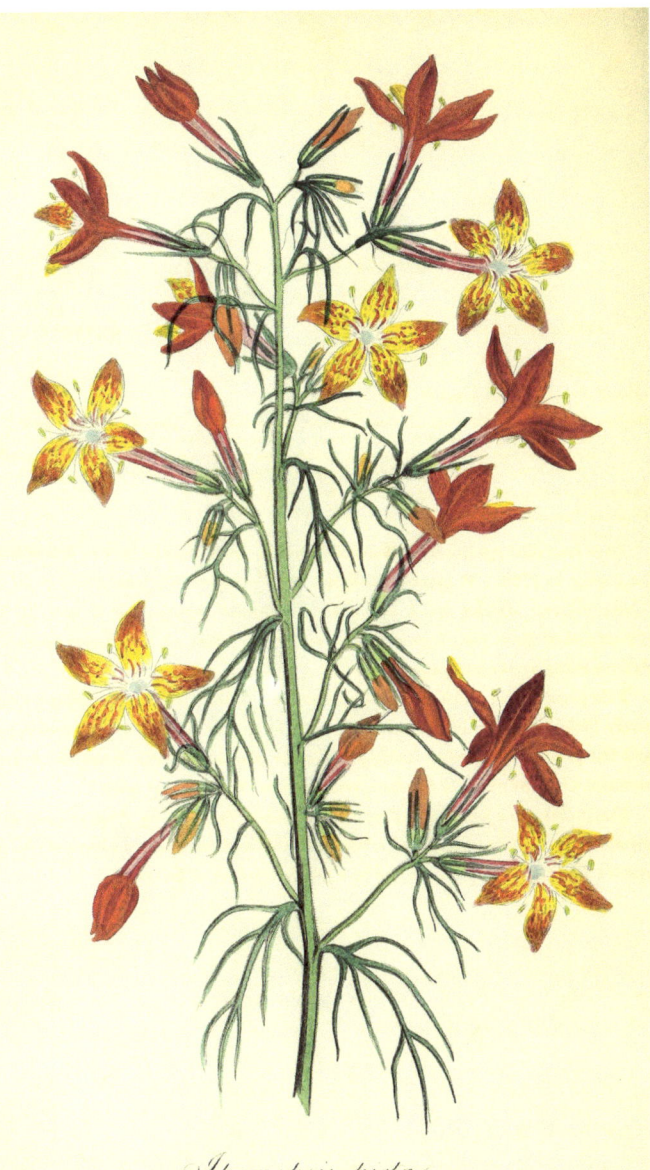

Ipomopsis picta

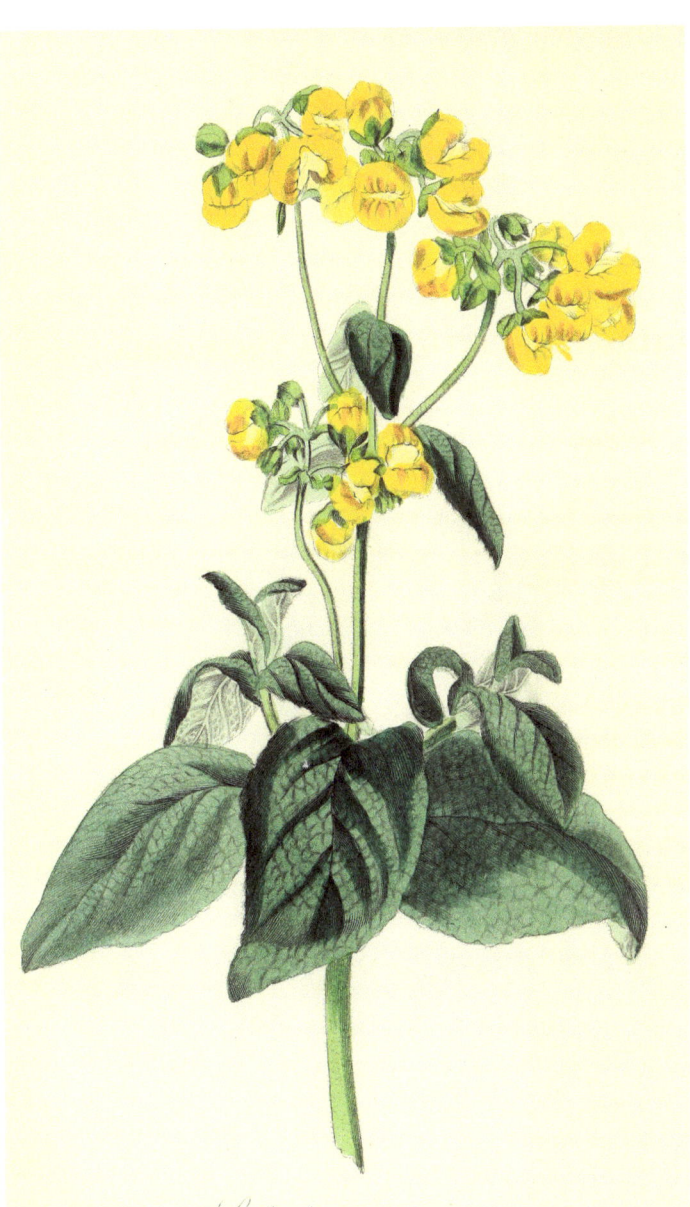

Calceolaria viscosissima

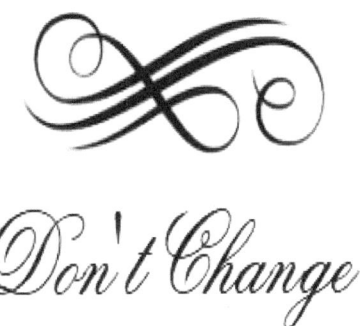

Don't Change

Don't change so people will like you. Be yourself and the right people will love you for the real you.

Unknown

For more antique and contemporary botanical designs, motivational quotes and more - printed and matted with free shipping, visit us at

www.BotanicalArtDesigns.com